Coloring Books for Adults

ABSTRACT SHAPES

Volume 2

A Wide Variety of Shapes and Styles to Discover

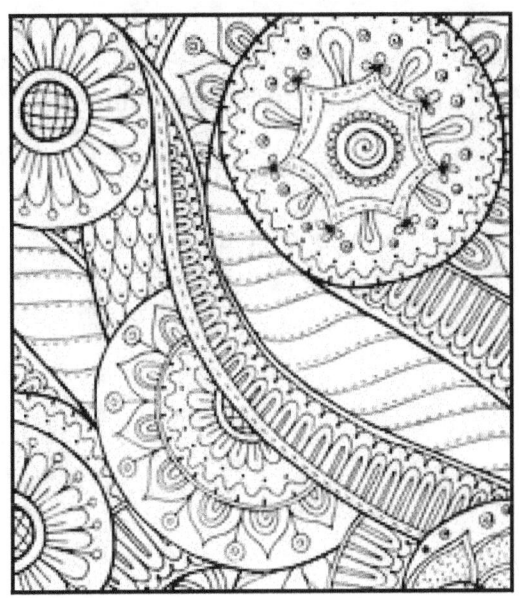

By: Asha Simpson

ISBN-13 978-1516995097

PUBLISHERS NOTES

Disclaimer

Paperback Edition

Manufactured in the United States of America

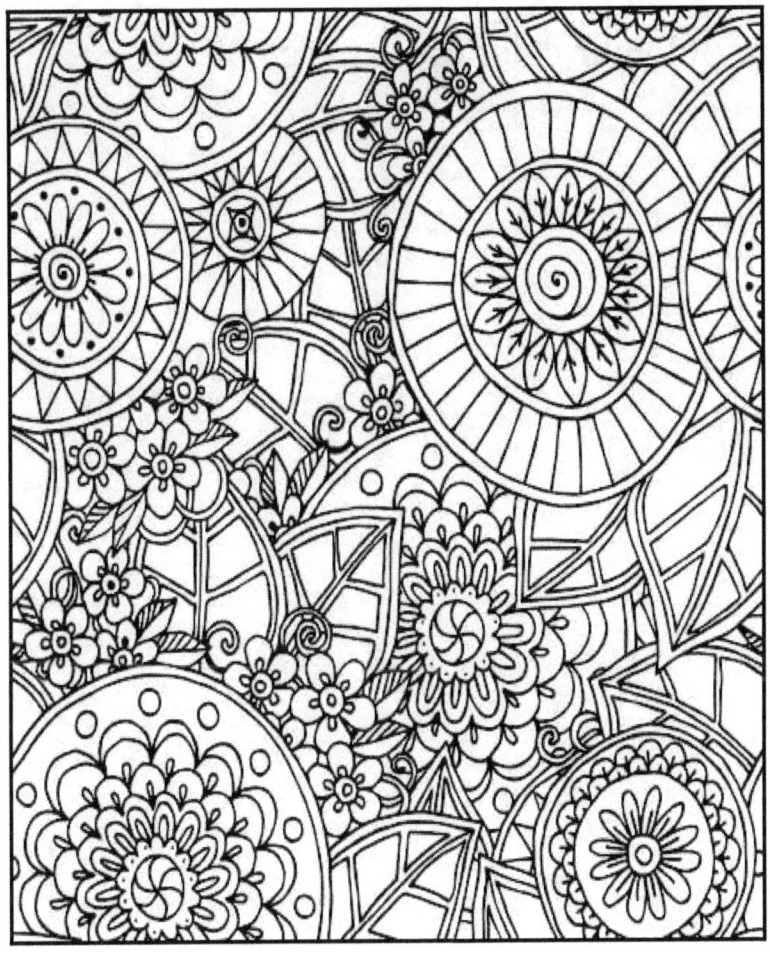

Try out your color ideas here:

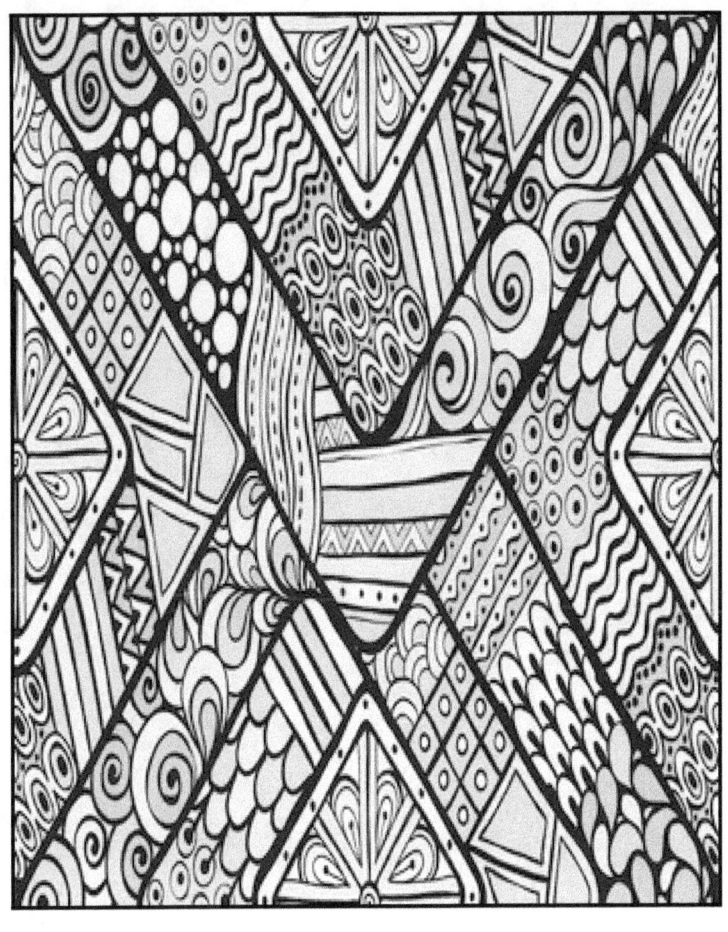

Try out your color ideas here:

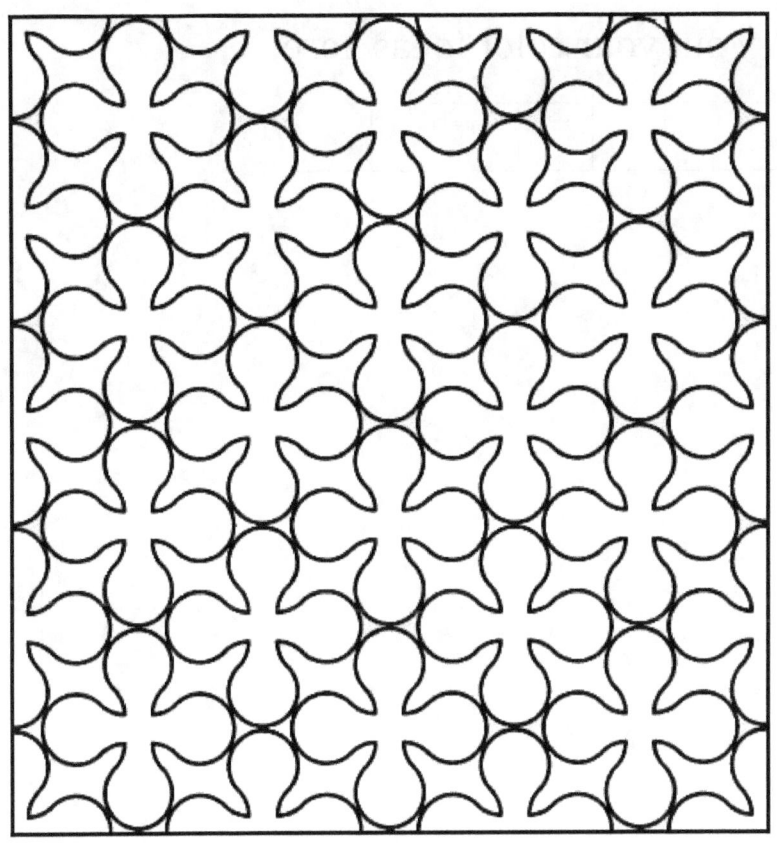

Try out your color ideas here:

Try out your color ideas here:

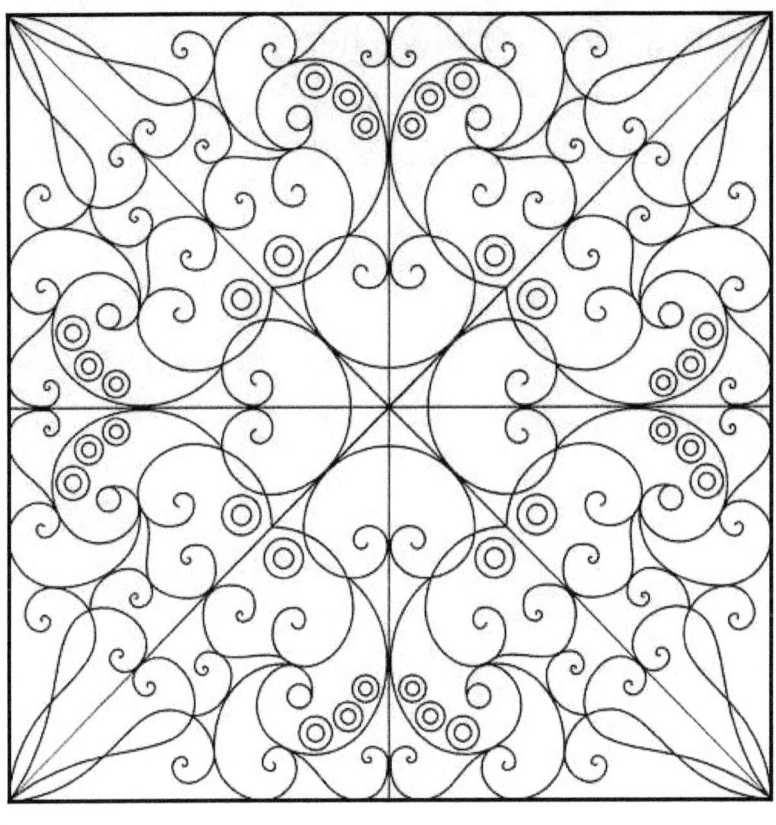

Try out your color ideas here:

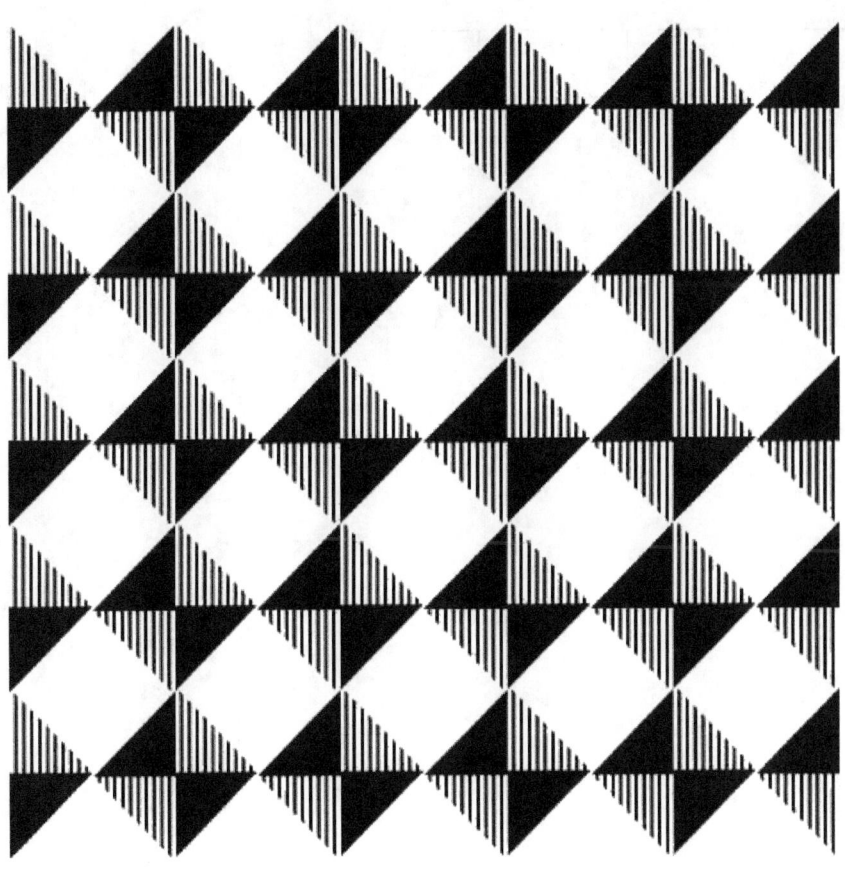

Try out your color ideas here:

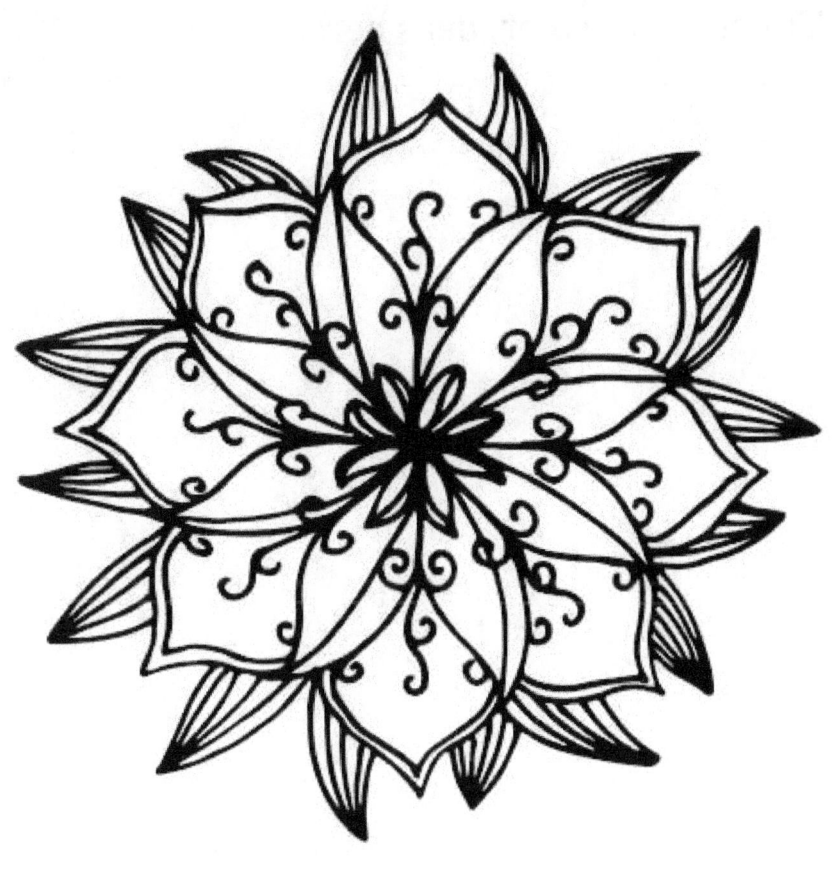

Try out your color ideas here:

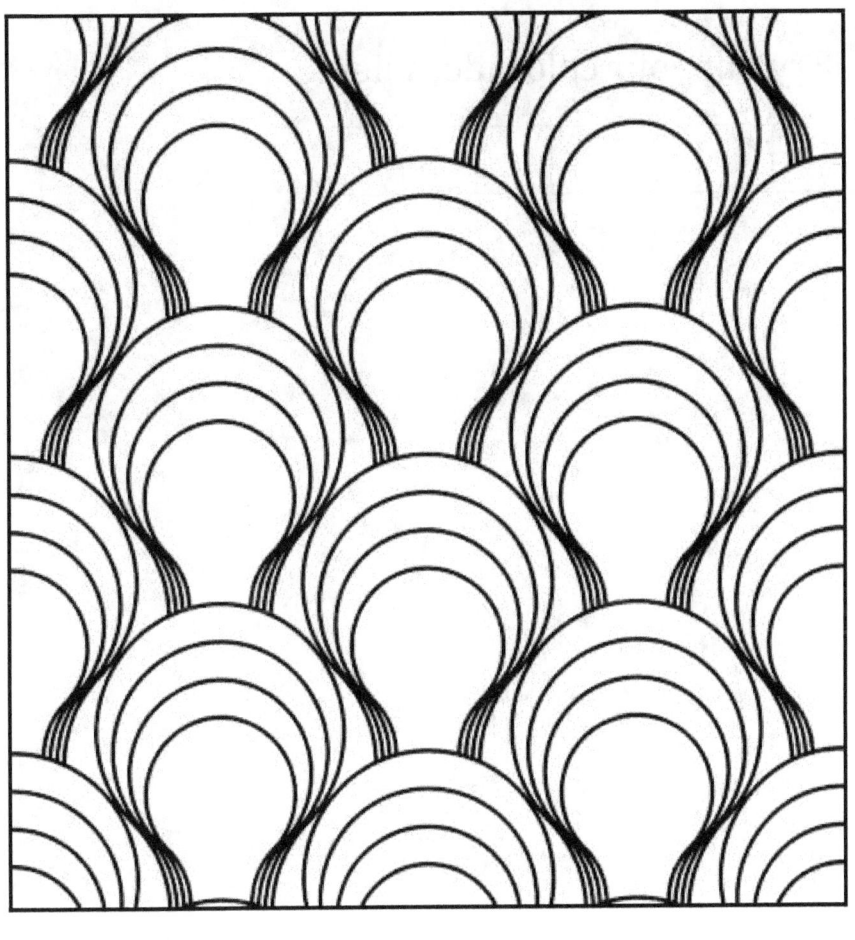

Try out your color ideas here:

Asha Simpson

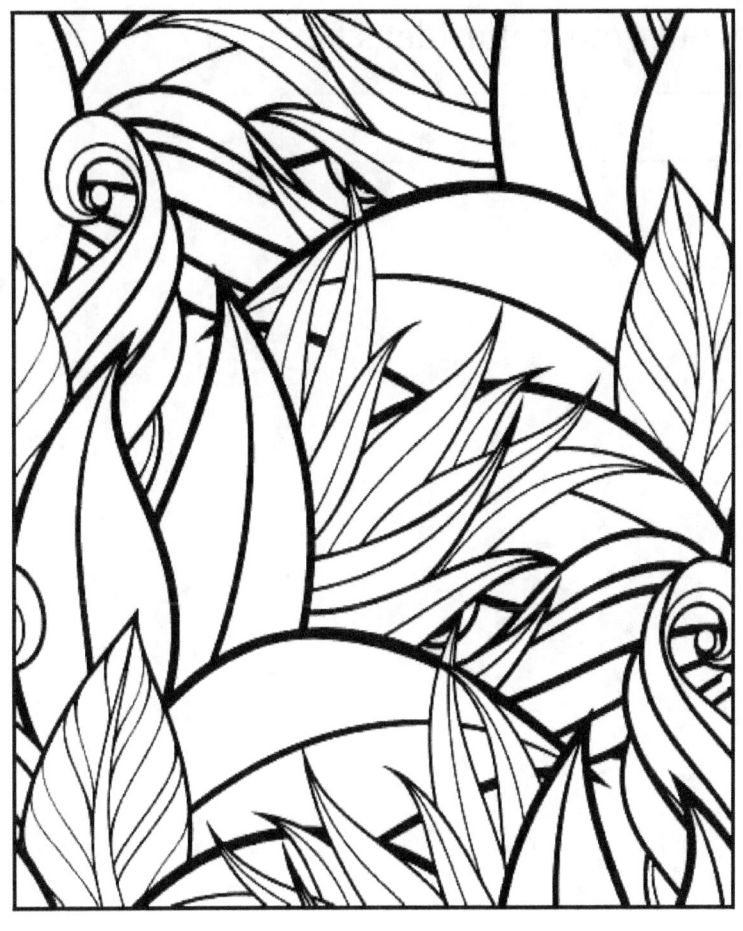

Try out your color ideas here:

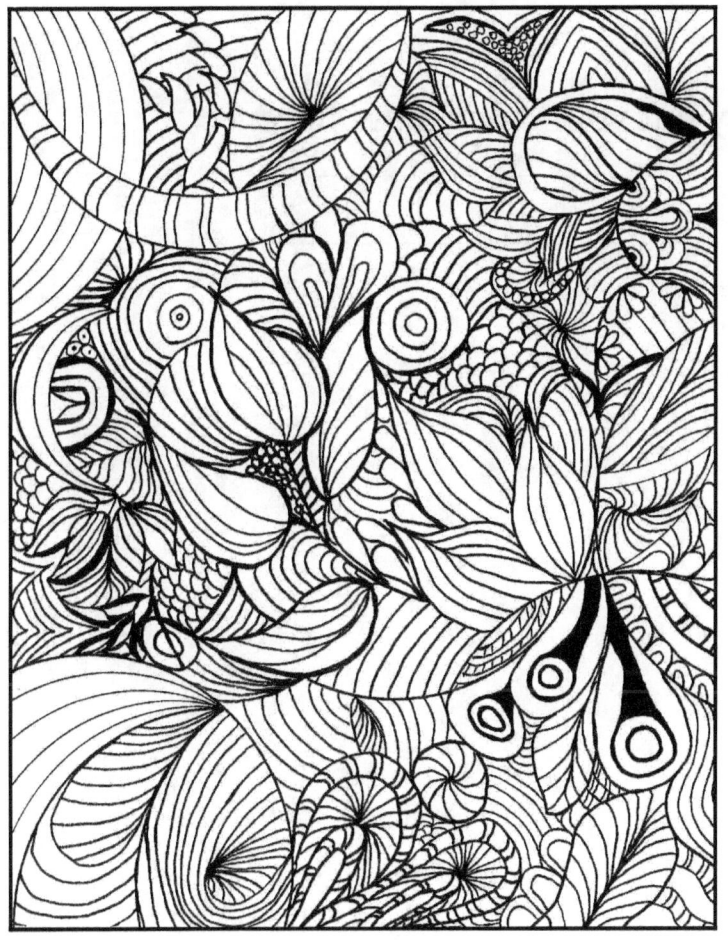

Try out your color ideas here:

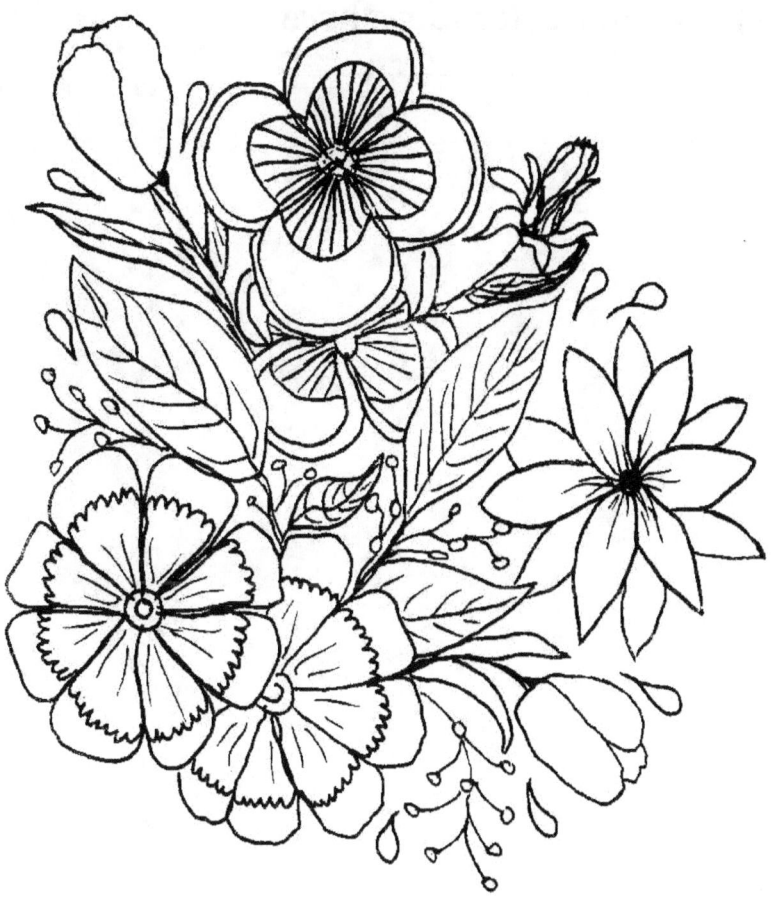

Try out your color ideas here:

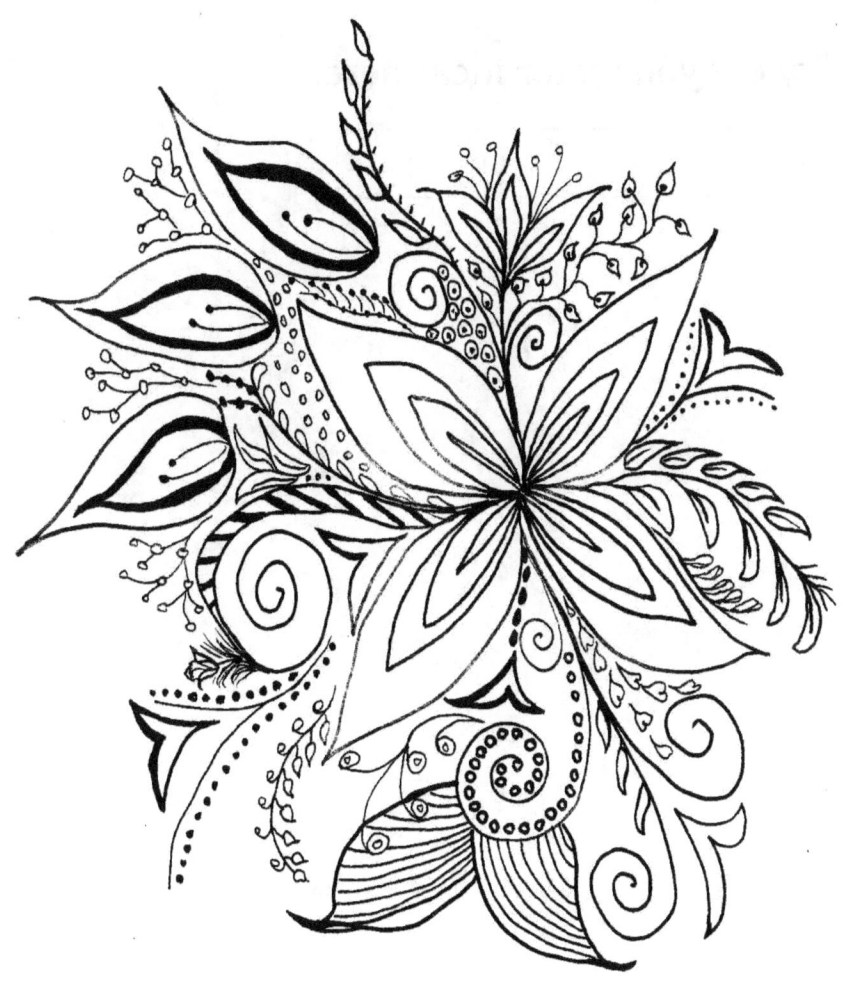

Try out your color ideas here:

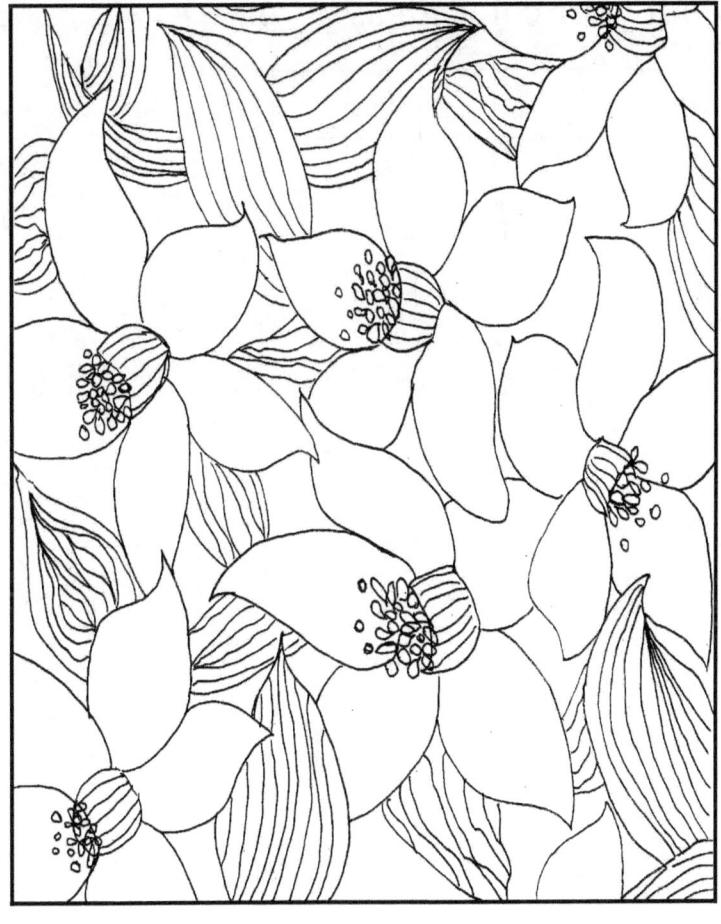

Try out your color ideas here:

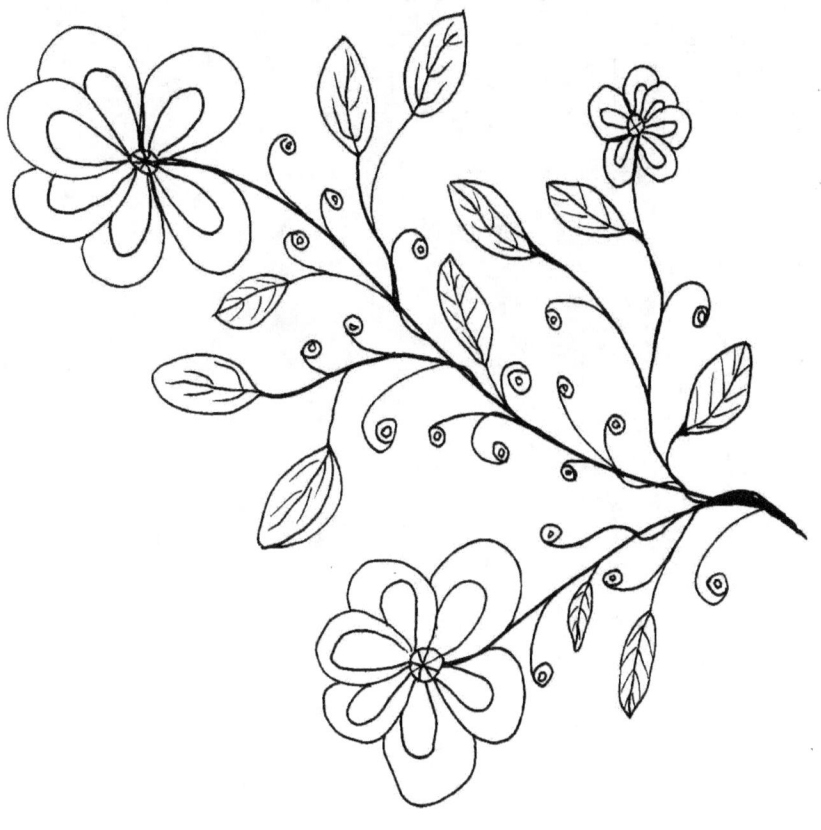

Try out your color ideas here:

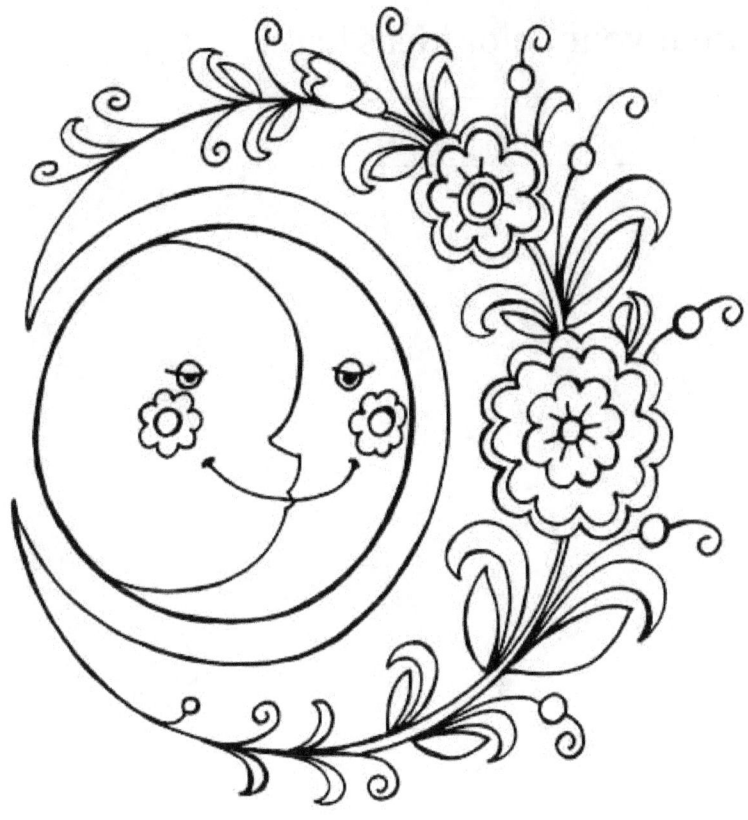

Try out your color ideas here:

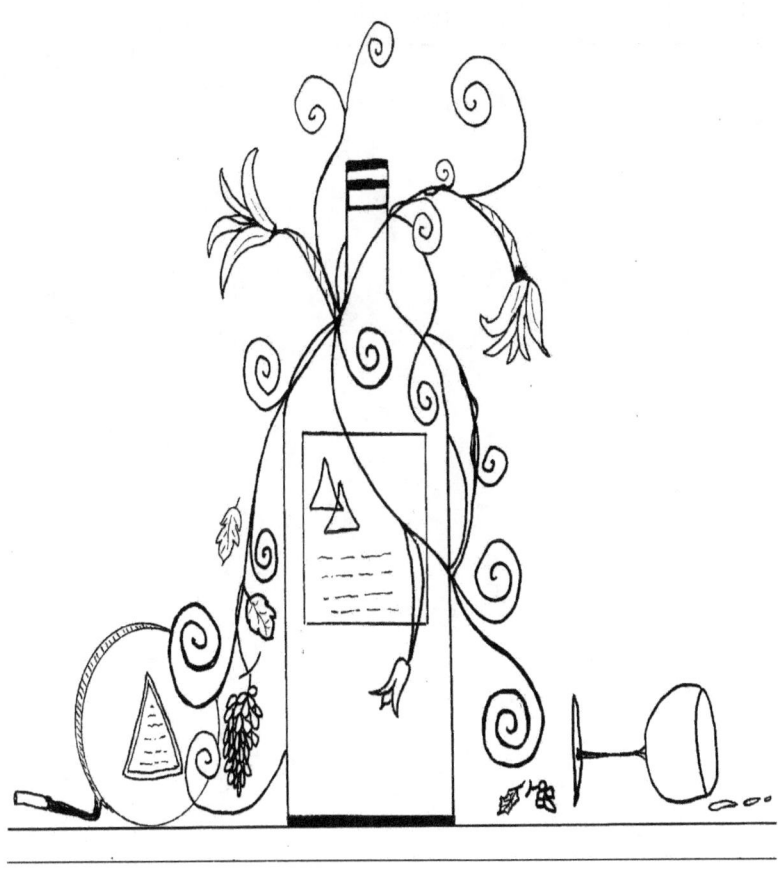

Try out your color ideas here:

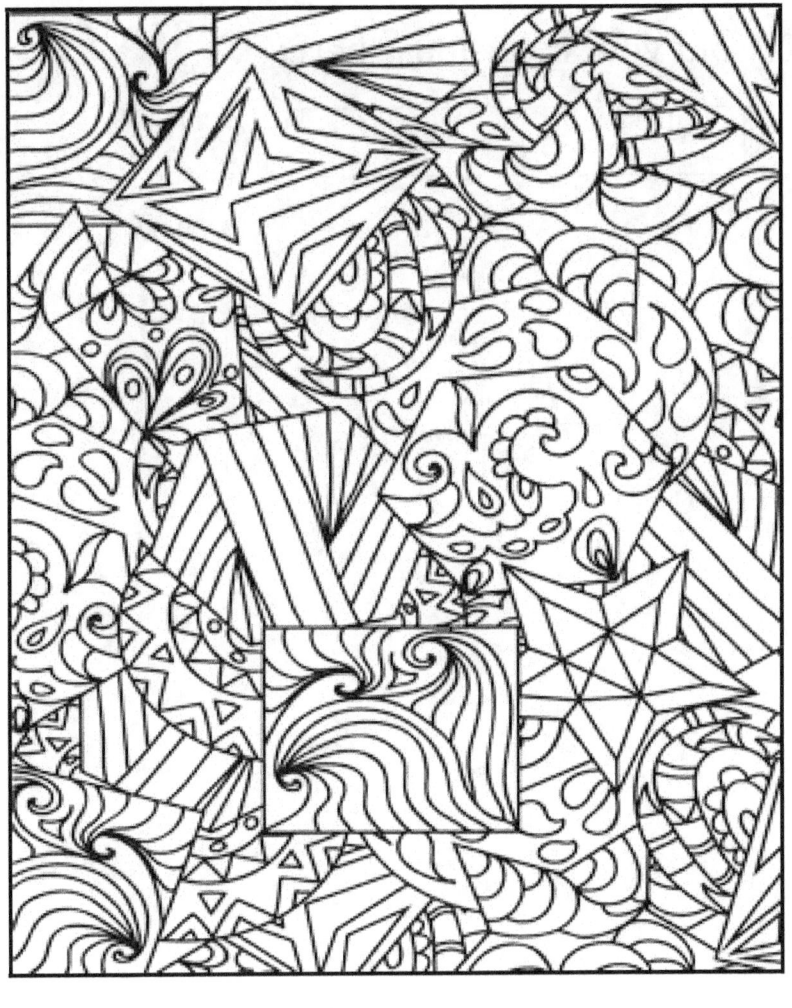

Try out your color ideas here:

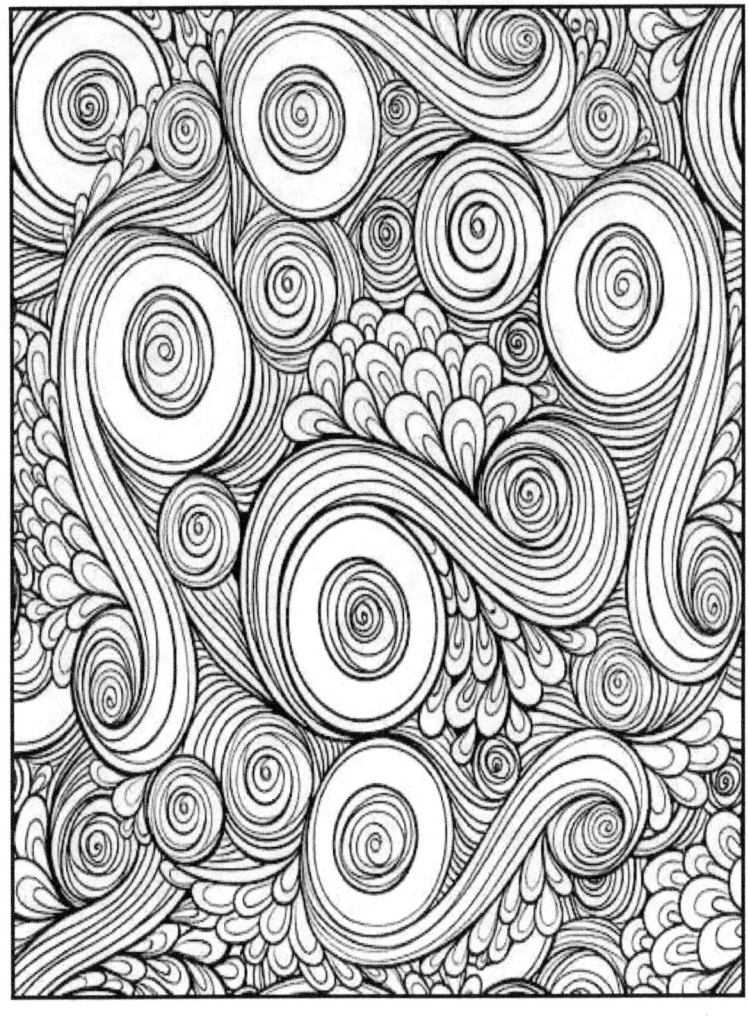

Try out your color ideas here:

Asha Simpson

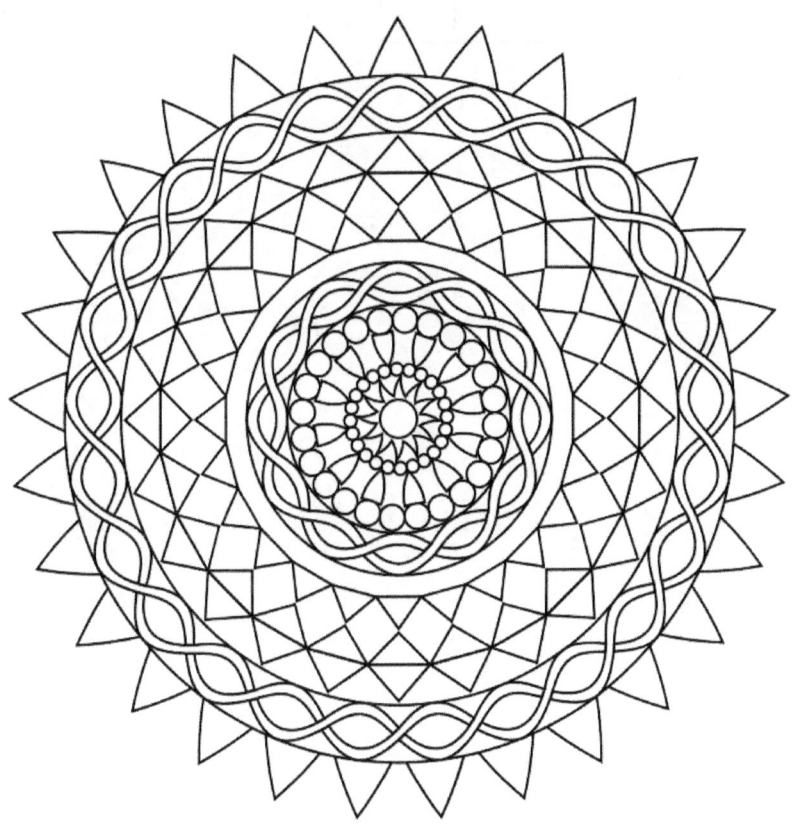

Try out your color ideas here:

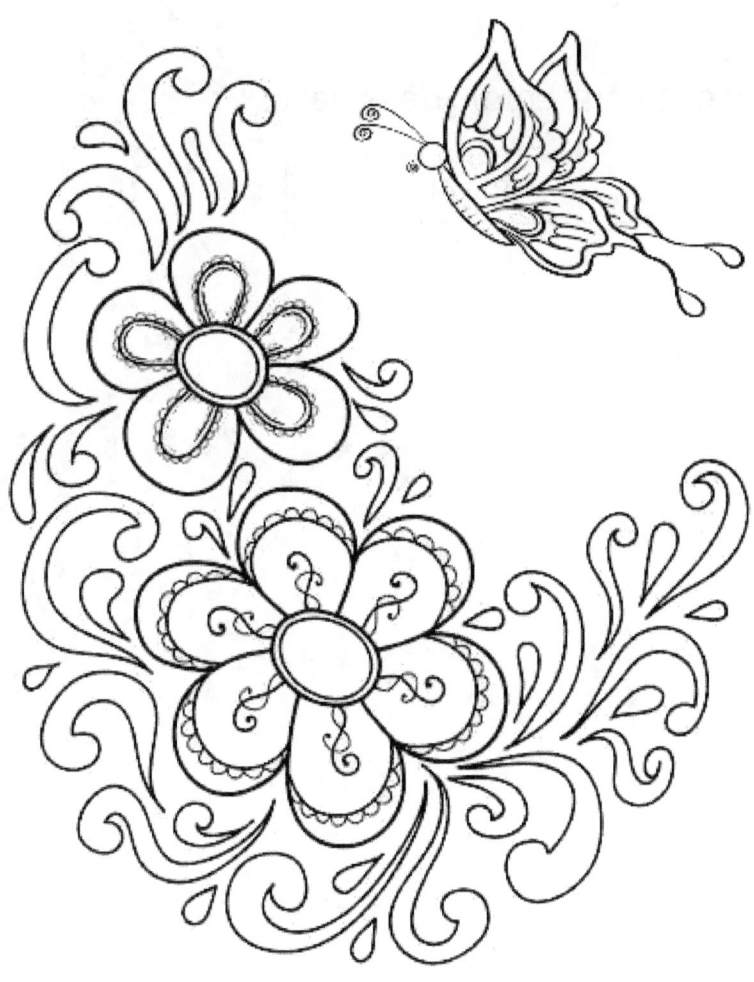

Try out your color ideas here:

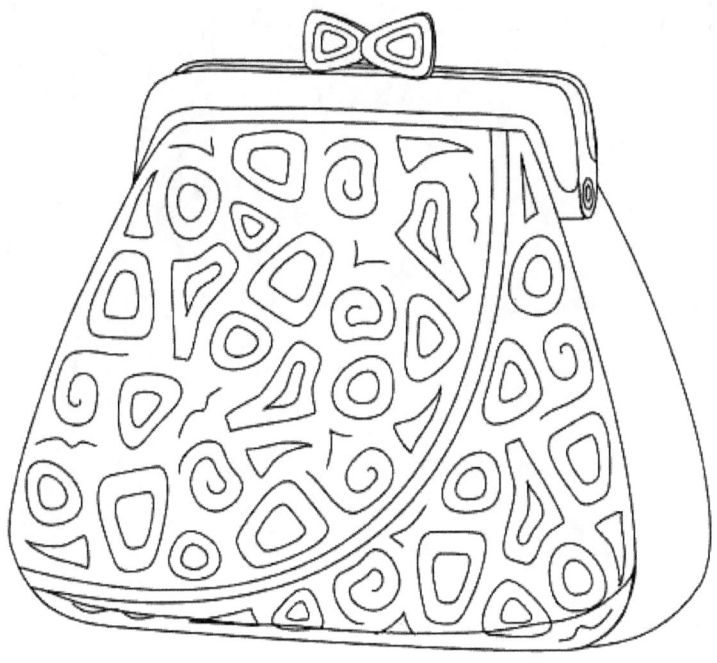

Try out your color ideas here:

Asha Simpson

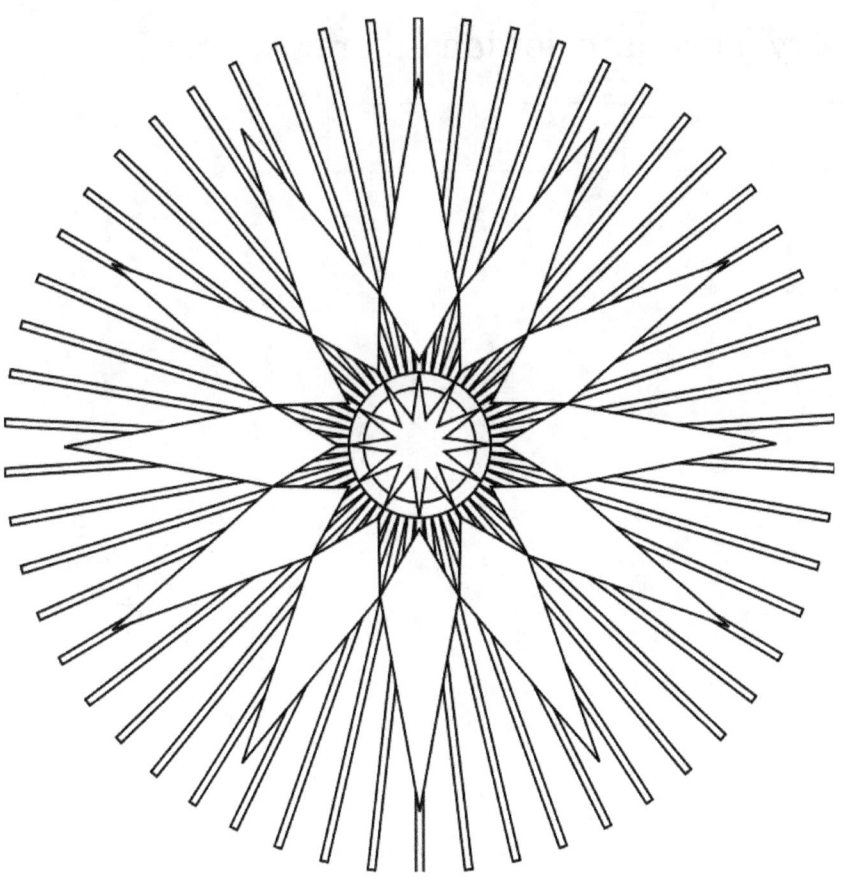

Try out your color ideas here:

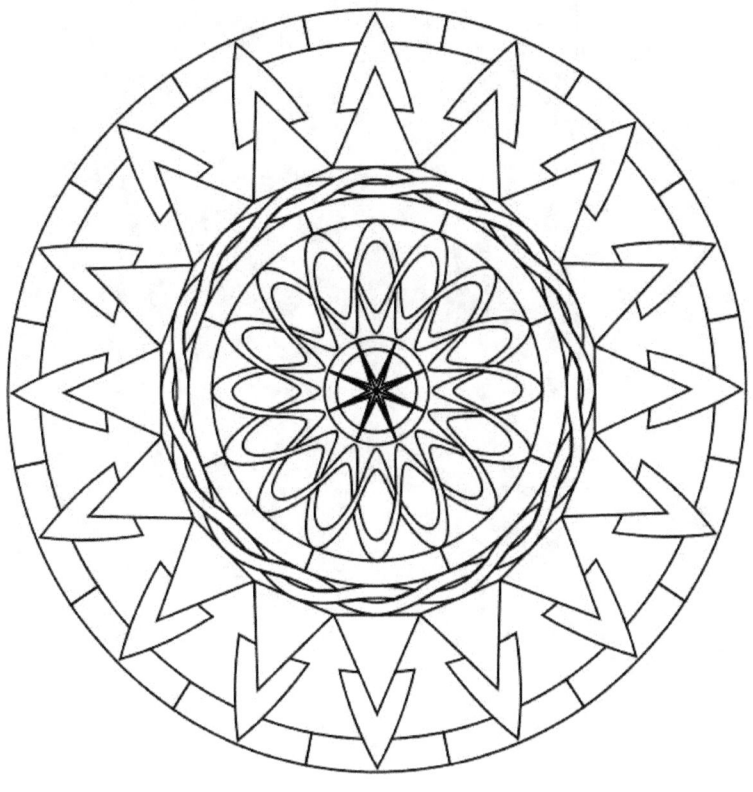

Try out your color ideas here:

Try out your color ideas here:

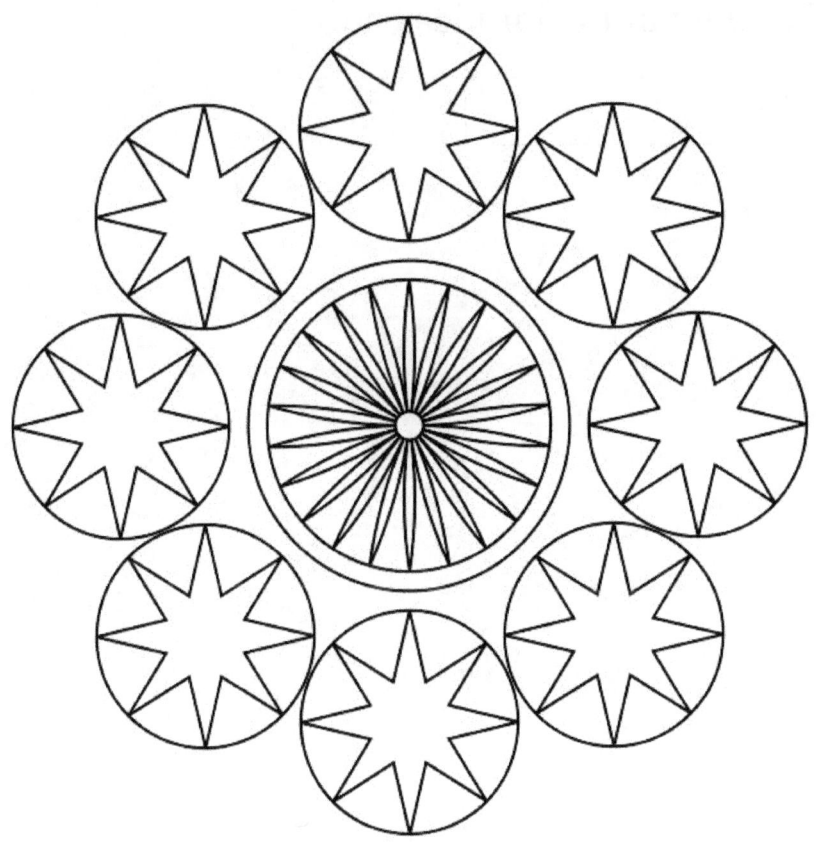

Try out your color ideas here:

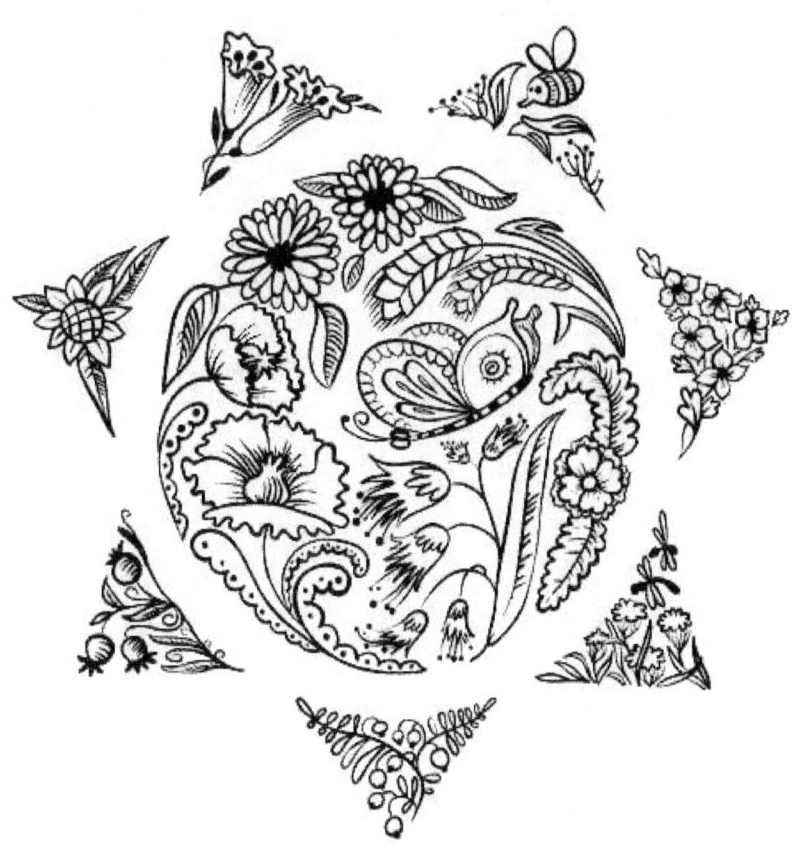

Try out your color ideas here:

Try out your color ideas here:

Try out your color ideas here:

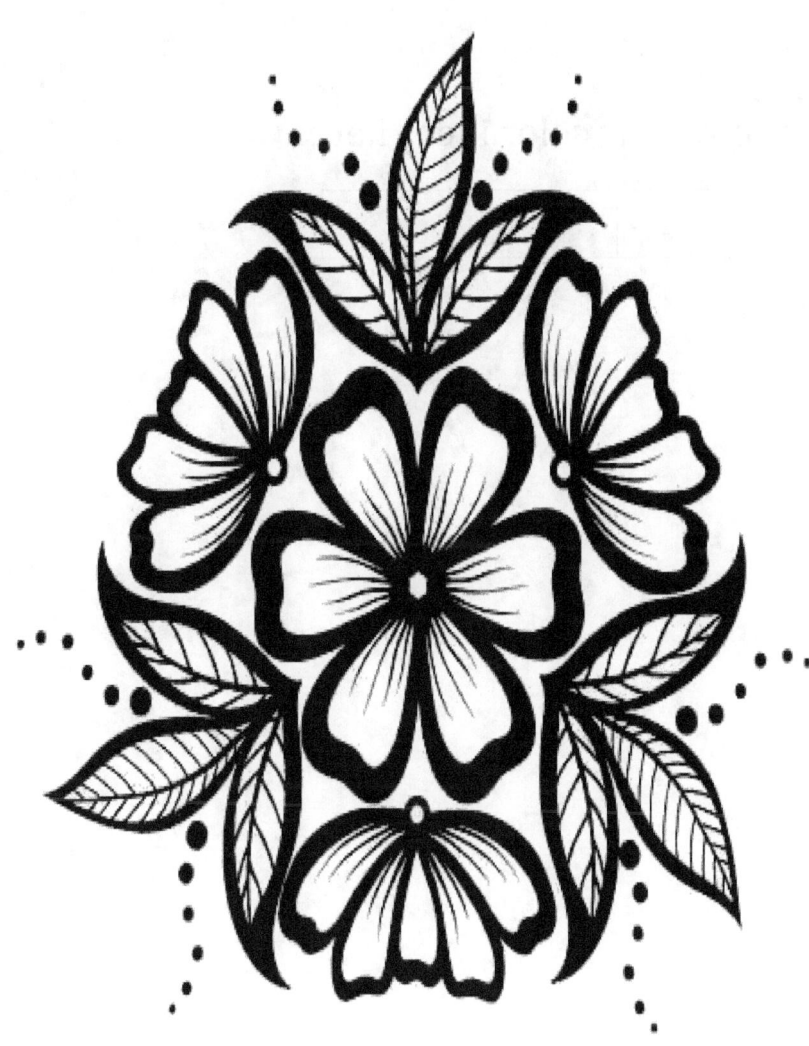

Try out your color ideas here:

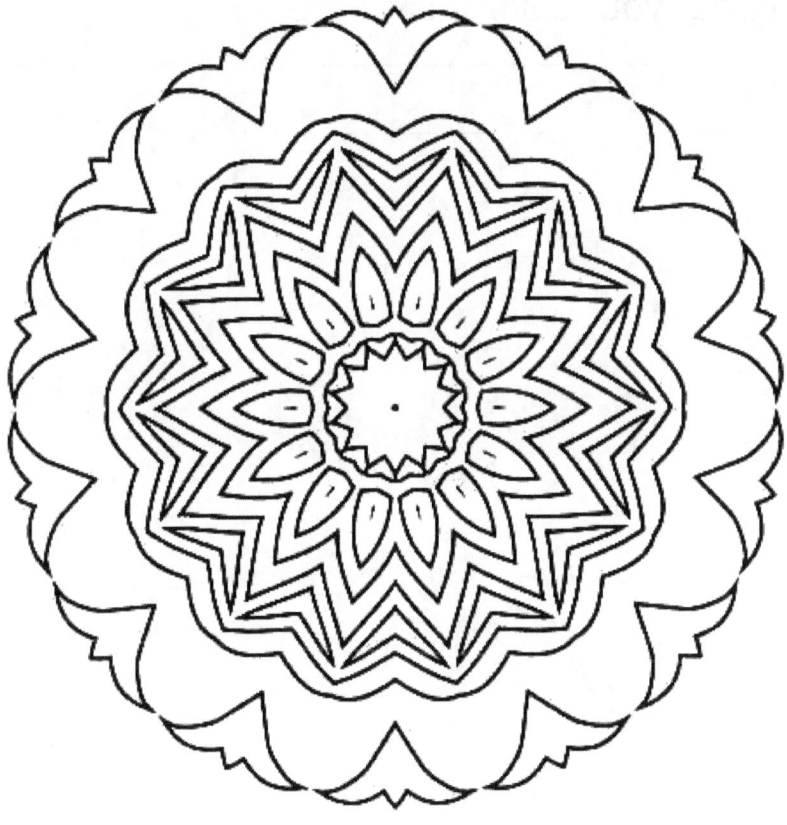

Try out your color ideas here:

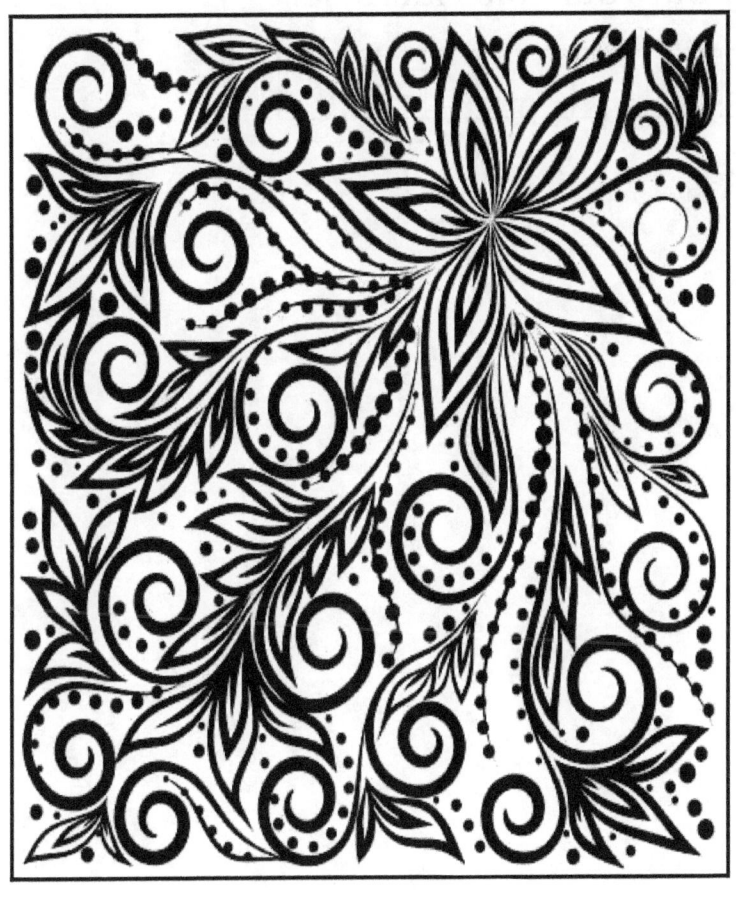

Try out your color ideas here:

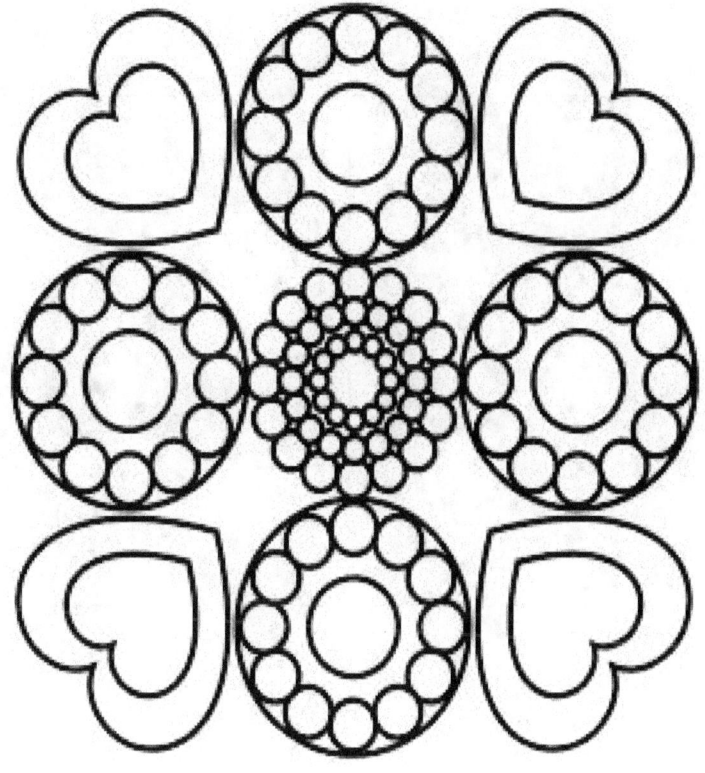

Adult Coloring Books -

Asha Simpson

https://www.createspace.com

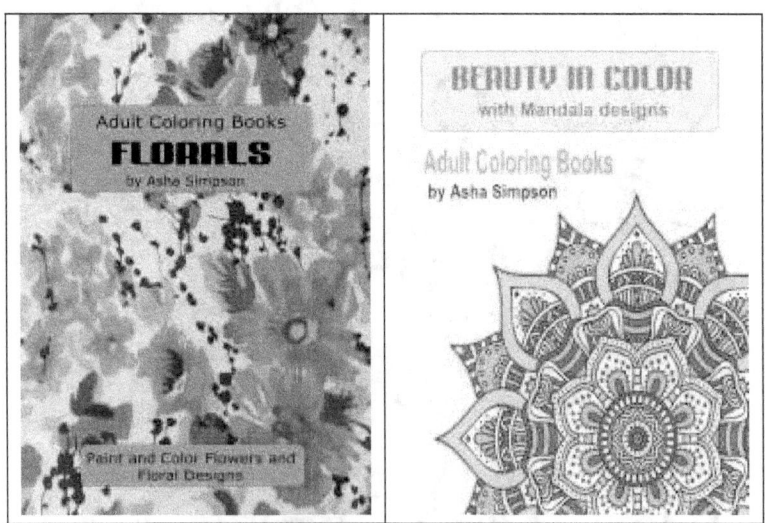

INFOEBOOKSONLINE

InfoEbooksOnline s a well known publishing company which specializes in lifestyle books of many kinds for both adult and children.

Their philosophy is:

Work hard and enjoy life through activities that replenish the body and the soul.

Paperback products can be sourced through

CreateSpace.com

InfoEbooksOnline.com

WordSearchandPuzzles.com